Drip Line

Poetry

Drip Line

Poetry

DAVID A. DREIBELBIS

Published by David Arthur Dreibelbis
Plainsboro, NJ
driplinepoetry.com

ISBNs: 979-8-9988474-0-0 (paperback), 979-8-9988474-1-7 (hardcover)

Front cover art and design by Molly Mortimer
Cover and book design by Mayfly book design

Library of Congress Catalog Number: 2025909226
First Printing: 2025

CONTENTS

THIS IS FOR YOU

Uncertain of the past, and afraid of the future . . .
Uncomfortable for good reason

Been there already, but not there yet . . .
Bored of the merry-go-round

Reading the situation, so unsure of yourself . . .
Ready for someone to come

DEAREST

You were born on a typical night,
But it wasn't the usual fight,
Their own advice doesn't work,
In the end, you're the jerk,
Unless you just tell them they're right

PAST THE BEND

You're always ready, to share some good news
A lifetime of loving, put yourself in their shoes

You know you can get there, if you try a bit harder
But with each attempt, the distance grows farther

You can't just ignore it, nothing quite works
Jumping through hoops. Only met, with smirks

You don't fit in their shoes, so why did you try?
Find your own size, and it's time to fly

For the Birds

I notice my feet, just past my stomach
Feeling the pain, eating is nice
Knowing fear, it's like ice

The ground is quaking, my throat is so tight
I see it clear, I am aware
I feel it, I prepare

My fingers are pinched, don't know if I can
So much of life, stuck in the past
My new feet, they came last

What lies in this grass? new strength with each step
I'm still walking, can I be free?
Now is my time, I will plant my tree.

DURING THE STORM

Wake up in darkness, the power is out
I think it's my place, am I meant to shout?

What will it bring me? Thick haze forms a ring
It's time for a try, this time I will sing

The notes echo loud, but not the right tone
As time passes by, my strains start to groan

Can't seem to escape, will my savior come?
He's meant to be here, my tongue's going numb

FOR THE BEST

Doesn't talk much, huh?
Must not have too much to say
At least he's breathing!

Still There

Old comfort with worn tracks
Shoes stretch larger each year
One day they stop fitting
It was already here

Old dark places feel new
Joy starts filtering in
You'll remember it all
With new strength, found within

By the Birds

Each morning they wake
And each night they rest
Minds stay aflutter
Remember the best

Feet not always grounded
Keep tending the nest
One day they will fly
With love, they are blessed

As the Sun Goes Down

Oh father who lifts me, why am I so heavy?
Oh mother who embraces me, why am I so cold?

Weary wings of hope
Strained breath to ignite

Fire pops
Tantalizing warmth and potential, sparks impossible to hold

They come when it burns
A constellation flickers black

Logs are burning
Bring yours, stars are rising

LOW FIDELITY

You figured it out, relief when it clicked
But not what we thought, just how you picked

New pathways found, not just the old road
Who else is out there, stuck with the same load?

They might want to join us, but probably not
They can't even see it, you'll give it a shot

Winter Planting

Peace won't be forced, that's frightening too
Joy starts to flow, when it comes from you

Don't forget who you are, when you're frightening them
The strength of your love, is only the stem

Warmth radiates out, but we still feel the need
You found what you found, but that's not their seed

STILL WATERS

Yellow light on dark walls
Laughter, in the next room
Mementos all around

A map of the world on the wall
While the fish swim in theirs

It brightens outside, just after rest

Time to go, peace can't be left in the nest

At the End of the Day

A life without space to notice what's there
The road laid before, never seemed fair

One day it's time to take steps for the best
Water the drip line, to help feed the rest

Definition

Drip Line[1]

1. a line on the ground where water falls in drops from roofs or the edges of trees

2. system of pipes that delivers water directly to a plant's roots (the parts that grow down into the earth)

Drip Line Poetry takes readers on an individual growth journey by exploring recognition, acceptance, and fresh starts. The poems inspire strength to move forward, past painful and unjust memories of betrayal.

In the end, joy comes from nurturing the parched roots of our own tree; with love, to bear fruit for our world.

---

1. "Drip Line." Cambridge Dictionary, Cambridge University Press, dictionary.cambridge.org/us/dictionary/english/drip-line